DATE DUE

Demco, Inc. 38-293

Bip

in

a

Book

Bip in a Book

story by **MARCEL MARCEAU**
and **BRUCE GOLDSTONE**
photographs by **STEVEN ROTHFELD**

Stewart, Tabori & Chang · New York

Published in 2001 by
Stewart, Tabori & Chang
A Company of La Martinière Groupe
115 West 18th Street
New York, NY 10011

Library of Congress Cataloging-in-Publication Data

Marceau, Marcel.
Bip in a book/by Marcel Marceau and Bruce Goldstone;
photographs by Steven Rothfeld.
p. cm.
ISBN 1-58479-130-6
1. Marceau, Marcel. I. Goldstone, Bruce. II. Rothfeld,
Steven. III. Title.

PN1986.M3 M29 2001
792.3'028'092—dc21
                                    2001034188

Printed in Singapore

10 9 8 7 6 5 4 3 2 1

First Printing

Designed by Nina Barnett

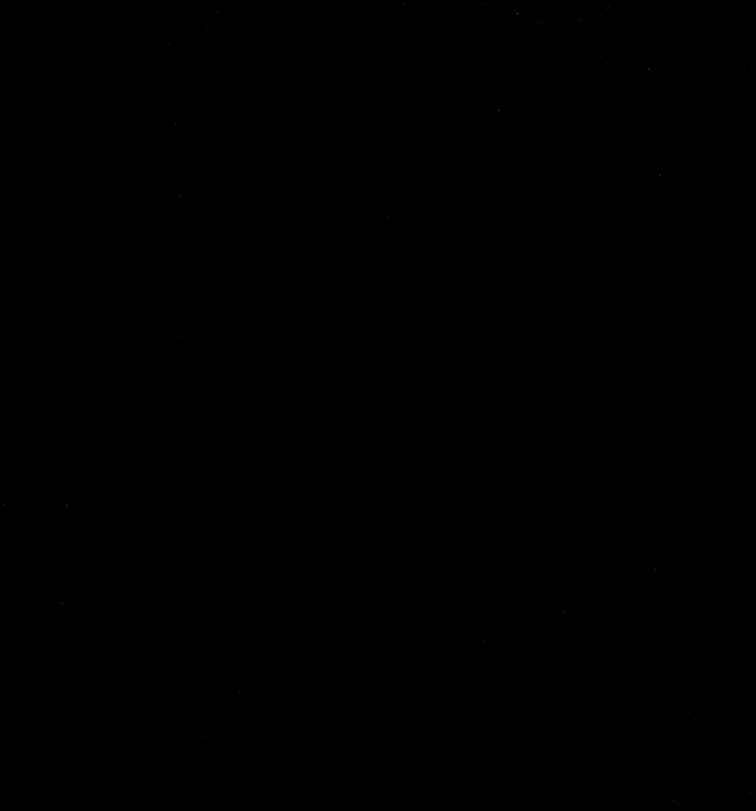

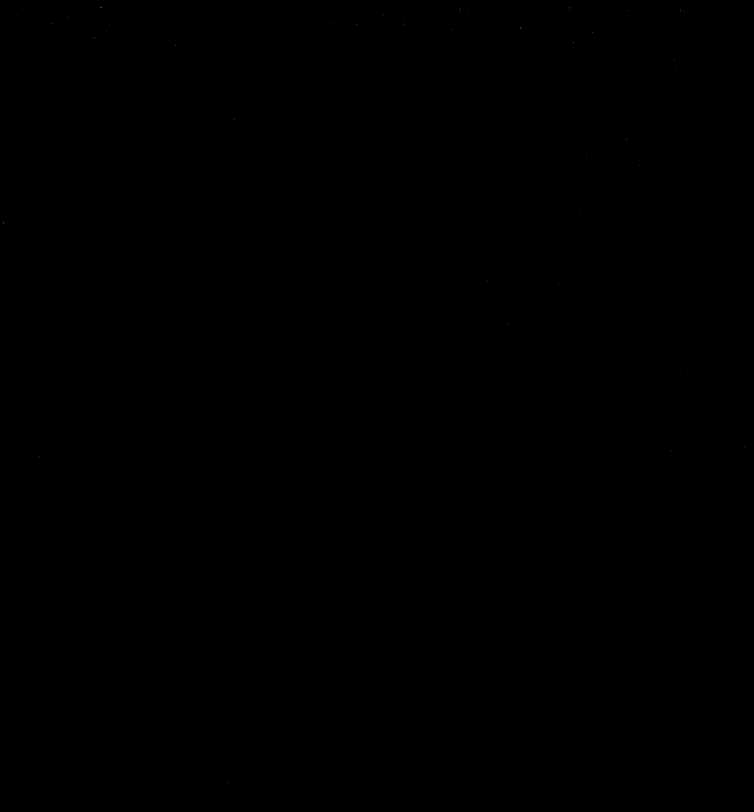

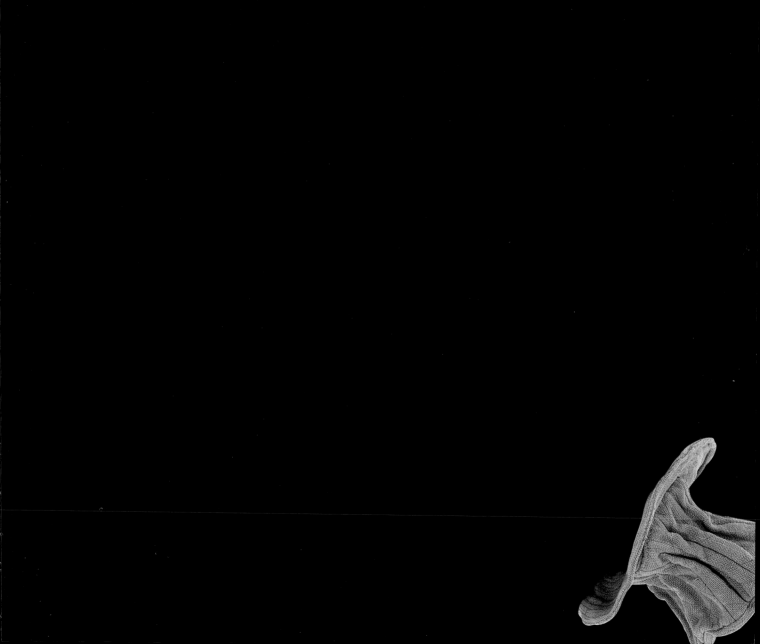

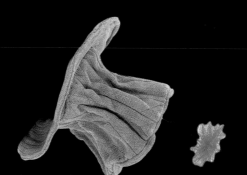

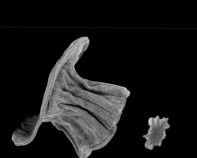